A message from · *Eine Botschaft von* · Un message de la part du

Dr. DAVID BELLAMY

From high notes in the 'O' Zone to 'Recycled Rag', it 'sounds green' to me too.
This is music swinging in the right direction!

Von den hohen Noten der 'O'-Zone bis zum 'Recycled Rag' klingt es grün auch für mich.
Dieses ist Musik, die in der richtigen Richtung 'swingt'!

Des nôtes dans les aigus de 'O' Zone à 'Recycled Rag', moi aussi je trouve que ça donne
une musique 'bien naturelle' – qui 'swingue' vraiment dans le bon sens!

© 1991 by Faber Music Ltd
First published in 1991 by Faber Music Ltd
3 Queen Square London WC1N 3AU
Music engraved by Sambo Music Engraving Co
Cover illustration and typography by John Levers
Cover design by M & S Tucker
Printed in England
All rights reserved

ISBN 0 571 51237 2

Sounds Green

10 jazzy pieces for keyboard on eco-themes

10 jazzige Stücke für Tasteninstrumente mit Öko-Themen

Une dizaine de morceaux jazz pour clavier sur des themes ecologiques

PAMELA WEDGWOOD

1   **In the 'O' Zone**   2

Ozone gases screen us from 99% of the sun's harmful ultra-violet radiation – the sort that causes skin cancer!

Ozongase schützen uns vor 99% der schädlichen ultravioletten Strahlen der Sonne – die Strahlen, die Hautkrebs verursachen!

La couche d'ozone nous protège de 99% des rayons ultra-violets destructeurs du soleil: Ceux qui provoquent du cancer de la peau.

2   **Save the Whale Waltz**   4

Thousands of whales are slaughtered every year. We must save the whale.

Tausende von Walen werden jedes Jahr geschlachtet. Wir müssen sie retten.

Des milliers de baleines sont massacrées chaque année. Il faut sauver la baleine.

3   **Lead-free lament**   6

Clear the air – use unleaded.

Reinige die Luft – fahr bleifrei.

Purifiez l'air! Prenez du 'sans-plomb'.

4   **Bottle Bank Boogie**   8

Take an interest – 2 million tonnes of wasted glass fail to reach the bottle bank. Just boogie on down to the bottle-bank.

Zeig' Interesse – 2 Millionen Tonnen an Abfallglas erreichen nicht die Sammelcontainer. 'Boogie' doch einfach runter zur Glassammelstelle.

Sensibilisez-vous! 2 millions de tonnes de verre sont gaspillés en n'étant pas recyclés. Alors ayez le reflexe container.

5   **Keep Cool**   10

Take the heat off the planet. Save energy.

Mach die Erde nicht heiß. Spar' Energie.

Coupez la 'chaudière terre'. Economisez l'énergie.

6   **Litter-bin Blues**   12

6 million tonnes of paper that we throw away each year have to be buried in a hole in the ground.

6 Millionen Tonnen Papier, welches wir jährlich wegwerfen, muß in einem Loch in der Erde vergraben werden.

6 millions de tonnes de papier sont jetés chaque année et doivent être enterrés.

7   **Rain Forest Fiesta**   14

In September 1988, fire destroyed an area of rain forest larger than Britain. How much will be destroyed this year? It must be stopped.

Im September 1988 wurde ein Gebiet des Regenwaldes von der Größe Großbritanniens durch Feuer zerstört. Wieviel wird es dieses Jahr sein? Das muß aufgehalten werden.

En septembre 1988, le feu a detruit une surface de forêt tropicale plus importante que L'Angleterre. Combien d'hectares vont partir en flammes cette année? Cessons là!

8   **Recycled Rag**   16

Why aren't telephone bills, gas bills, electricity bills, circulars and all music books printed on recycled paper?

Warum sind Telefonrechnungen, Gasrechnungen, Elektrizitätsrechnungen, Wurfsendungen und alle Musikbücher nicht auf recycled Papier gedruckt?

Pourquoi ne pas imprimer sur papier recyclé les factures de gaz, électricité et téléphone, ainsi que les prospectus et les livres de partition de musique?

9   **Green is Beautiful**   18

It is our duty to care for the countryside – be aware, safeguard it.

Es ist unsere Pflicht, uns um die Landschaft zu kümmern – sei wachsam, erhalte sie.

C'est notre devoir de protéger l'environnement. Soyez conscient. Sauvegardez là!

10   **Rock-on Wildlife**   20

Thousands of wildlife species – animals, birds, insects – are under the threat of extinction. They can never return.

Tausende von Naturarten – Tiere, Vögel, Insekten – sind von der Ausrottung bedroht. Sie werden niemals wieder zurückkehren.

Des milliers d'espèces – animaux, oiseaux, insectes – sont sous la menace d'extinction. Ils disparaîtront à jamais.

In the 'O' Zone

Save the Whale Waltz

With sadness ♩ = 108

Lead-free Lament

Bottle Bank Boogie

Keep Cool

Litter-bin Blues

13

Rain Forest Fiesta

Recycled Rag

Green is Beautiful

Rock-on Wildlife